STORIES ON COUPONS

STORIES ON COUPONS

ALL 2 OF US UNDERSTOOD

Caroline Macleod

ISBN: Softcover   978-1-6641-1433-3
             eBook   978-1-6641-1432-6

Print information available on the last page.

Rev. date: 01/21/2021

To order additional copies of this book, contact:
Xlibris
UK TFN: 0800 0148620 (Toll Free inside the UK)
UK Local: 02036 956328 (+44 20 3695 6328 from outside the UK)
www.Xlibrispublishing.co.uk
Orders@Xlibrispublishing.co.uk
825178

CONTENTS

• • •

2 REBIRTHING LIFE

L. Schreyer, P. Klee and W. Kandinsky formed the triangle at the Bauhaus.

Schreyer and Klee moved in with each other because of the process of arts they discovered together.

Independent consultant of friends. They discovered the tri-color.

Schreyer, He came from knowing what the Christian circle is. Faith, It determines our life choices.

W. Kandinsky and P. Klee were the best of friends.

Personally, I find Klee and Kandinsky joint artwork personality perfect.

Now you know how to make a masterpiece.

35 BARCA

• • •

Thy Kingdom Done
Thy will be done
Hassan The Bull.
Islamist and Christianity meet here.
ONE is in capitals or entities lower case.
Wear All. The love is in the burning bush Inn fire.

And when you come out of indoubt of insecurity your shallow feelings
go smaller in love.

WarGold.

It was 1112/13. Frank French RIP. Saw the incidence in the Channel
in 1918.

Everything is all about sex, money and love.

Well there is an end to infinity then as Klee Bauhaus said, along with
Kandinsky. 2and 2 is 4 and goes back to stop.

BATON G FLAT

• • •

Stoccato is represented by the double CLEFFE.

Trumpet comes in and viola and cello play a ring of 5. Plus 3 straight and one low to high tone.

Hitler destroyed the World for the love inside himself to be itself. A man will do that for his love in himself because he likes to be in control.

BEGGAR

• • •

Murder

Someone sets a mental soul to murders with a laying. (LAY-ON).

Usually we have 5 hidden souls 3 of which are physical and 2 of which are mental in a man and 3 of which are mental in a woman and 2 of which are physical in a woman. (USUALLY).

USUALLY all we need to do is to realize we have this disturbance in ourselves. (PURSE).

Usually it will disappear from us then. Intimately emotionally.

No guilt involved.

It comes back to the 5 words filtered down through 5 generations again where a word is said in error and gets casting.

It's natural collapse point of view whether the activator or the victim.

We are putting things in our pockets to kill ourselves then;
Expand on the idea of scent's cover-up and what it costs us physical at the same time as taking our money.

To teach and how to learn; to teach some of them want to be cutting. Some of them want to be abuze to teach; Beggar not to be told to be Simon Sez.

BULLYING

Consiousesse's are halved when a problem is shared and this is good enough for the idea of e'sh-scharrings's.

It is a school secret among lee-ways. The school is a big playground. Indecent unsolicited behaviour is common-place.

This is because of Law buying lee-ways of school playgrounds. This happened in the 1970's.

Rupert Murdoch:Do you think anyone is anything because anyone is anything? So you turn the reckless irresponsibility into something positive to feedback your own-selves's pense. Looks like it's come from the SS NAZISM. From some peasant. Would you rather have me homes-schoolings you? No, I'd rather go to school and escape for the day.

DEATH

· · ·

If you hand yourself over to a power greater than yourself it's alright. Amen because it is biblically so.

DIARY 1

• • •

Cut down wine consumption.

It's the following year and I have not cut down wine consumption.

We met a young man facing the cold alone - so took him back to ours.

Don't know why the heating is not fixed.

Told to send a letter to the next place only it's got soup on and not sure how the response is going to be.

Never heard.

Shower runs cold because hot water not switching on.

Doom and gloom as we realize we have lots of work to do for the young man.

Got a bed problem - mattress is too thin.

Nice boy - really determined.

It's so easy to turn around and go away and leave everything in a particular way because it's human nature to not to go forwards.

I am the master of my own death.

I am not the Master of my death nor am I the Master of my life.

Totally freaked today.
Had my own mini-episode.
Muddled up about everything.

Thought I had to get out.

Phone call to discuss help.

Suddenly realised then I did not want to go at all.

Got the best flowers ever. Clever man.

On a Monday be alive and Tuesday will begin another day.

I am in love with George and always will be.

I'm frightened and feel a sense of doom as does George.

Sunshine has warmth in it today. Lovely.

Eat well - it's better than drink. Don't want to be an old soppe.

I meant us to have too much. In the way I wanted him to be a man
and to pay me back for it.

Disgraceful. Fishing sold to Europe and we buy back their old sea deep
fish.

Cars Cars Cars. A continual normal argument from my childhood.

I get my Company by the weather, the energy and beauty.

Reflections of light on the Loch are included in my Life friends.

The cold acceptance into my body is exhausting.

The Warm is a blessing of Love from the sun.

The changes are friendships that last for Life Long.

Woke up this morning to the constant ring of the phone at 6.00am.

Decided to take all the bottles to the bottle bank and later decided to stop drinking.

No cat food in the local shop until Wednesday. Got what I could.

Had a good sleep in the afternoon. Feel rested.

Stopped the wine today. Feel sad but okay. I'm not going, it will be better.

Sort of got there with bills this month. Maybe I will not need a tab at this 4 weekly period. Happy to think of this.

I smell of an onion shop.

Money is the darnedest thing then.

Mid-evening and not dark yet!
Yippee.
Warm Day.
Happy.

Have George my band back.
So married in name and love which suits everyone.

Much as we have spare.

We had to have a car but then it was unnatural to have a car?

Taken from us away?

Have George a row this morning for being cheeky.
Sorted now. Cleaned up the table and so did George.
Emptied the Rose petals and put the fish on the wall.

Better now. Things have calm again.

Too much on the phone. He's a worrier. Finding it hard to wake up too. Impossible.

Love George. Nags me but I am sure of his returning love. Tersed at by family.

I am not Gil with people. Just like to say hello with a joy wave.

I feel like George is moving on and I get scared at being left isolated alone.

All I have left is Faith. I have realized my faith and I am humble. Up and down.

DIARY 2

• • •

George and I don't owe each other anything anymore.

Period's of menstrual cycle changing.

Peeing my knickers suddenly on laughing too much.

Bit of hassle about driving. George being eyed up.

Am I strong enough?

Rang Landlord about inner doors and backdoor with cat flap. Not available now.
I'm glad all round.

Had thoughts about Christmas dinner today. Think I'll just follow the general course of what's happening this year. George was saying we will spend it at home. Love him.

Finished my face today! 14 years. 3 facials.
Washing only now and it can go to relax again.

Happy this morning.
Woke feeling well.
George concerned at my lack of sleeping for getting up too early and then crashing out at afternoon.
Feeling alert.

Woke happy this morning. Lots of energy.

Swiftly cleaned the house re-organising.

Finished jobs for large furniture in the house. A few soft furnishings to arrive.

Really do love my George's, it's just too many rapid eye movements.

George's birthday today. 62. I feel more stable now a lovely feeling of secure main stay.

Darling George has a new version of himself now and feeling happy again with relief. Kind, loving and charming. As always.

Been on a spending 3 weeks. Halejuliaah it comes to an end now.

Bought a dream.

Happy Retirement.

EAT

. . .

Vegan have bean not meat. Cheese is called porcini. Mushroom is called porcine. Onion is not possible with bean.

Vegetarians do not eat fish. So are strict more than vegan. Vegetable does not mix with eggs.

Lacto Vegetarians should stay away from lacto products.

When washing up, glasses first, mugs second, cutlery third, plates fourth and pans fifth.

Napkins/Serviettes it's up to you.

Red wine chilled or room temperature.
White wine chilled or room temperature.

Black and white harlequin floor in the bathroom.

Front room sofa day bed.

Plastic furniture white in the garden.

Light cutlery.

Pretty plates.

FLU 101 PHILOSOPHY

Spanish flu first occurred in 1918 and 101 years later has returned to exactly the same level of infection. It was not reported how it stopped, just that it petered out suddenly.
Greek yoghurt/marscapone, soured cream, crème fraiche with a little wood soot/peat/moss.

Dow Jones industrial was hit by United Nations and Ban Ki-Moon. It was Then for the Wall Street Crash in 1929.

So we all know what we are doing now then.

Britain has trade deal with European Union. Successful.

Accept feelings for happy in a stressed situation comes with guilt association. Until realized freedom of being perfect unit gregarious.

Women are prerogative.
Men are Civilized.

GAMMA

• • •

It's the Bastards religion. The only thing that can upset Bastards religion is GREED.

I think president TRUMP has woken up to this now.

NORDIC COMPASS NORWEIGIAN: NSSWS (SEX).

Mr Alan Ben, ken clark and Micheal Foot with Michael Helseltine (German), introduced the coco-cola-ban in the 1970's due to the English Mafia in Spaghetti Junction.

Heart matters;(LOVE).

5 to 2 then 5 to 3 to 2 then 2 back to 5 through 2. Changes pulse rate up and down.

A Droite and a gauche mean, "the same thing". Thing is le truc. It's Queen Catherine moorish. That's Y the British men acted like they did that then In Syria. Time 50 years ago. SYRIA Persia. Coming of understanding is better for GOD. Whatever happens. It has come from Reason. HALLAS. ALLAH I understand from my Prayer-time in SAUDI ARABIA on a rooftop Riyadh at prayers.

121.2 in hundreds. X3 = thrupence (MONEY) works more interest to pay. So reduce VAT to 17.5p forevermore. 5.27 8ths makes a diamond. 5 13halfsths makes a crown. Don't worry it's all like official secrets act.

It is all revent. This world has many incredibly different facilities.

Lesbianism has been made a monkey of.
Gaye men have been made a Fish of.

HERINE

. . .

One day Luc remembered a Fri-end who he realised had to pay for a punishment to someone else who demanded payment of a physical kind as well as payment in the price kind.

He was, he realises the someone who was paying for the punishment of the then all in part of the process normally.

There were two ways to pay. Introduction of someone and laying it onto him.

Rescuing him from it all was an older woman.

In between was the act of violence.

Just like the many divisions in the Christian faith there are many differences in the Bastards religion where knots and all knots appear therefore supply and demand hold ups.

INDIA

• • •

India space program needs a little less attention. If we are flying people to stratosphere then we have found all the information we need already and probably quite a few years back.

Concentration of people who need a room for a family in great demand for 1p a fortnight.

Let's sort out our planet first.

China is in great shape.

Lost all the sandalwood trees in Nepal, let us send our money through via their to India.

LOSS

• • •

The 6th Law. The degrees of loss.

This explains LOSS.

This is why 9/11 and why Whom.

The 12th Amendment. The Twin Towers were brought down by the monetary fund IMF.

It Then.

The 5th amendment and the 8th Constitution are represented in the picture by a Book.

The 9th amendment. Badness. Leaves behind traces of its presence of three threads; indeciety and precise and precious astralls. The 3 hidden of 3 are the astralls:Stars in our eye's then.

Badness is paid for why, as, monetary fund IMF.

Badness leaves behind TWO CANDIDATES, the Occupier's and the Buyer's.

Badness leaves behind the people who buy it.

Badness is perfect. Do humu sappiens understand perfect? No.

It is totally normal Bias romantically.

LOVE

. . .

Carry was her name and she said life is a cycle of violence and castigated though.

Five words and three words take us through the cycle of our lives.

We can see clearly if we want to.

Sometimes we don't want to because of law and morals which use ethics to allow lawful war.

I have chosen to accept the way of life.

It is not possible to change law on war because it is in a circle of church and war ethics.

To blackened have us from time to time and leave us remonstrants to abide with yew.

Accept at thee that time.
or:
accept at that the Time.

Two choices for two different people.

Pick one gold, two acceptance of time.

Time immemorial when you have picked what's right for you as yew.

Yew protects you from spirits casting shadows over onto you into your etherialities.

MOLLY

All is well and all shall be well.

Molly thought about this and here following is her story.

She knew it was on death when you went to the Lord, a power greater than yourself. Normally handed over by your own spirit.

People are okay, she thought.

On going so does she.

Visit the brook she remembered her story of the hedgehog signalling pathways in your brain.

She had asked to be rescued by the bear and he had helped as best he could. Was she deserves to be helped? She wasn't sure.

Could she have been stronger to have helped more herself? She didn't want to understand everything.

Totally up to her.

NICE

To speak to someone rather than to talk.
To relevance Church to a dictatorship only.
To ask essential questions not too deep and pray.
To be a courtesy when you want to help and then only.
To have love and obey then give all you want to.
To help and not too help for gratification of yourself.
To be appropriate to a current situation in your own capacities.
To be adventurous with yourselves and let them fly freely-free.
To like what you eat and not too eat just for praise.
To be loyal but not below voluntary servitude.
To say to know something whenever it appears to you but not before.
To sense some other people's gratitude and in appreciation of it give yourself away.
To be appreciative of best times and worst times and dull times because it's a full life.

PAINTING

. . .

I paint Pachaise.
I paint flowers.
I am Caroline Macleod.
I have painted the mountains of this landscape.
I have eeries and celebrate.
Flesh and flowers.
Water and air.
It is offset and a misplacement.
I am semi-pro.
It is Individual Simple style.
I visited the Picasso museum in Antibes and took a clue away with me.
I looked at a Japanese screen and learnt evility.
Art history is the rest of my style.
Practice and saying "what", is the rest of it.
Colours are a mystery board that start with your own knowledge.
My paintings are clay, simple plaster painting, deep set painting.

RATIO

. . .

Since last July 2020 all deaths in the United Kingdom are attributed to Covid19 deaths.

There are a ratio 2:1.

SCOT

• • •

And Scotland learning another trick of the trade, fishing quotes don't matter.

And Taylor is Scottish. HRH Prince Andrew escapade.

2 pence in the lb of fish is important. Over 5 years we would see our Country dissolving quite naturally. We need to change law2a and to effect it immediately to the fishing rights of this country. With regard to our community.

Clerical Error:
Pence and pounds:. No.
Pence and weight. Yes.
However it is called pence and waiting.
Ukraine nevermind.
Ukraine Country code is 12.
It is an easy mistake to make.
Britain would not do anything for it because of a trade trademarks union.
Donald Trump has a mother from The Isle of Lewis. That's probably why he asked for help in the elections.
Our Country code is 14.

South Korea is American and they are dissolving metal in Yuki bath's instead of dissolving plastics in Yuki bath's.

UNITED NATIONS

. . .

Black people have their dominance in numbers and we have our dominance by the power of their dominance.

I like Black people and have gone out with them.

I like everyone because of self-love.

I like self-acceptance in general and in-course in everyone.

VARIOUS ASSORTMENTS

• • •

There was a woman who had such ire in her through being childless that her anger made her kill a room full of people through a child.

Law being the way it is made the child carry all her children for her.

The child didn't want to sink in the swill of it so she came to know it's alright fighting her way straight through it all.

VINEGAR VINTAGE

• • •

A raspberry dinner is wear'e you eat something vinegar and tell her to him what you have intent to do to her for to him.

When people dying breed the most discontent to us we are really only interested in the loss of our relationship with them as they are still living but in another sphere. Some people can still contact them but whether we have faith in the tellers too us is our own luck. You can either make it for yourself or not.

That's the flamenco kissing 'till your passionate strutt stocatto. It is to sing Flat.

I was given teacher training in Lypiatt becose that was all I was going to be.

At Christmas the song/written words' of And a away in aye Manger, saddened people BECOSE it is such a poverty poor birth of Christ masse Jesus with presents in a Manger of an Angel which requires 3 kings to guide it. Gold colour and Frankincense and Myure, which relates to the benefits of poverty and we are all fed literature of money means love in success.

Actually it's a very rich birth.